Lenten Bible Study Series B

Study Guide

Ken Schurb
Richard Shuta

SAINT LOUIS

Edited by Thomas J. Doyle

This publication is available in braille and in large print for the visually impaired. Write to the Library for the Blind, 1333 S. Kirkwood Rd., St. Louis, MO 63122-7295; or call 1-800-433-3954.

Copyright © 1999 Concordia Publishing House
3558 S. Jefferson Avenue, St. Louis, MO 63118-3968
Manufactured in the United States of America

Contents

Introduction

Session 1: The First Sunday in Lent   7
            God Does Provide!

Session 2: The Second Sunday in Lent   14
            Losing Life to Find It

Session 3: The Third Sunday in Lent   20
            Wise in Christ

Session 4: The Fourth Sunday in Lent   26
            The Focus That Inspires Hope

Session 5: The Fifth Sunday in Lent   32
            In Giving Is Glory

Session 6: The Sixth Sunday in Lent   38
            The Master's Mind

About the Series

This course is one of six Advent-Lent adult Bible study courses. The Bible studies in the series are tied to the three-year lectionary. These studies give participants the opportunity to explore the Old Testament lesson, the Epistle lesson, and the Gospel lesson appointed for each Sunday during Advent and Lent.

Each course will draw you deeper into those parts of Scripture that deal with some of the greatest events in the life of Jesus—His incarnation and His passion. Although these courses may be used any time of year, they were originally designed for the two most reflective seasons of the church year: Advent and Lent.

Each study is designed to help participants draw conclusions about each of the lessons appointed for a Sunday, compare and contrast the lessons, discover a unifying theme in the lessons (if possible), and apply the theme to their lives. The Leaders Guide for each course provides additional textual information on appointed lessons, answers to the questions in the Study Guide, a suggested process for teaching the study, and devotional or worship activities tied to the theme.

May the Holy Spirit richly bless you as you study God's Word.

Session 1

The First Sunday in Lent

(Genesis 22:1–18; Romans 8:31–39; Mark 1:12–15)

Focus

Theme: *God Does Provide!*

Law/Gospel Focus

The Christian life is not an escape from troubles, hardships, and temptations. Where there is no conflict, there is no opportunity to conquer. God calls us to repent when we doubt His ever-present power to sustain us in all our needs. None of our present struggles is greater than God's love for us in Christ. Through Jesus' faithful sonship, God has provided both a safe standing in the presence of divine judgment and sure victory over spiritual enemies.

Objectives

That by the enabling power of the Holy Spirit working through God's Word, we will

1. acknowledge that God has loved us enough to provide us with His Son as our substitutionary sacrifice for sin;
2. trust that Christ's perfect obedience continues to provide us victory at all times over temptations, troubles, and hardships; and
3. rejoice that, due to Jesus' victory over temptation, nothing in time or space can separate us from God's love in Christ Jesus and the eternal life He provides to us through faith.

Opening Worship

Sing or speak as a litany the following stanzas of "Savior, When in Dust to Thee."

> Savior, when in dust to Thee
> Low we bow th' adoring knee,
> When, repentant, to the skies
> Scarce we lift our weeping eyes,
> Oh, by all Your pains and woe
> Suffered once for man below,
> Bending from Thy throne on high,
> Hear our solemn litany!
>
> By Thy helpless infant years,
> By Thy life of want and tears,
> By Thy days of sore distress
> In the savage wilderness,
> By the dread, mysterious hour
> Of th' insulting Tempter's pow'r,
> Turn, O turn, a favoring eye,
> Hear our solemn litany.
>
> By Thine hour of dire despair,
> By Thine agony of prayer,
> By the cross, the nail, the thorn,
> Piercing spear, and torturing scorn,
> By the gloom that veiled the skies,
> O'er the dreadful sacrifice,
> Listen to our humble cry,
> Hear our solemn litany.

Introduction

A ship proves its value not in dry dock, tied to a pier, but by the way it survives amid turbulent ocean waters. "Man is born unto troubles like the sparks fly upward," said Job (5:7). It does not take human beings very long to realize that cuts and scratches and testing and temptations litter the path of life. Likewise, it is only by passing through the challenges of life that the Christian experiences the truth of God's promises to provide in Jesus safe voyage to His heavenly home. For the Christian, clouds do not all have silver linings, but behind the clouds the sun always shines. For God has given us His Son as our sacrificial Lamb and Victor over sin.

1. Share a time in your life that could be described as "turbulent waters."

2. How did God sustain you in the turbulence?

Inform

The three lessons for our study call us to trust in the God of love who has provided in Jesus Christ all that we need to receive His eternal blessings.

Many people regard Genesis 22:1–18 as the most remarkable story in the Old Testament. It is referred to as a "type," a foreshadowing not through words, but through deeds. It parallels God the heavenly Father's action of providing His Son as the sacrifice to rescue sinners. Scripture teaches God's eternal and unchangeable plan of salvation for all people. Abraham's willingness to sacrifice Isaac paints a most striking shadow-picture of a God who loved the world so much that He gave His only begotten Son as the sacrifice for sin.

In the Epistle lesson, Romans 8:31–39, we learn that despite the many struggles against our sinful flesh, the God-hating world, and the power of demons, Christians will be victorious because they are united to Jesus. His love for sinners has gained certain victory for them.

The Gospel lesson, Mark 1:12–15, briefly tells of Jesus' temptation (more detailed accounts are found in Matthew 4:1–11 and Luke 4:1–13). This account is consistent with Mark's theme of

Jesus as the heroic and obedient Servant of God who willingly does battle with humanity's chief enemy, Satan. Jesus is not like ancient unfaithful Israel in the wilderness. He is faithful and obedient. In Him, God now begins His creation of the new Israel. At great personal cost, the faithful Son of God triumphs over the foe. Jesus thereby insures His people their spiritual inheritance. He Himself is the heart of the "Gospel," the Good News that brings us back to God and His rule within the human heart (the kingdom of God).

1. There are several parallels between the story of Abraham's call to sacrifice Isaac and the account of Christ's Good Friday sacrifice. Recall something in Jesus' life that parallels the Old Testament lesson:

   a. Abraham's only son Isaac was born as a result of a miracle. Jesus …

   b. Isaac carried the wood for a burnt offering up the mountain. Jesus …

   c. Isaac made no attempt to escape. Jesus …

2. How do the two accounts differ? (See Romans 8:32.)

3. What words in Genesis 22:12 are echoed in Romans 8:32?

4. When Isaac asked, "Where is the lamb for the burnt offering?" Abraham said, "God Himself will provide a lamb for the burnt offering." Was Abraham's reply an evasion or a clear statement of faith? And if of faith, then faith in what? (Consult Hebrews 11:17.)

5. This side of eternity, Christians are often viewed as losers still struggling with sin, or as mere survivors. Yet what are we really? (See Romans 8:37.)

6. Who drove Jesus into the wilderness to be tempted? Why is this important?

7. As Jesus was about to begin His public ministry, He showed that He would carry it out in such a way as to accept a shocking event Satan sought to have Him avoid. What was the event? (See Romans 8:32.)

8. The Holy Spirit does not stop our Adversary (the word "Satan" means "adversary") from buffeting us with temptations. So what is the "Good News" that Jesus preached? (See Romans 8:33, 34, 37–39.)

Connect

1. Share with the group an experience in your life in which Satan tempted you to doubt that God would provide for you or tempted you to think that there are "shortcuts" to happiness?

2. What common occurrences can be used by Satan as temptations to disbelieve in the goodness of God? (See Romans 8:35–36, 38–39.)

3. The quest for self-esteem is a hot topic of books and talk shows. What phrase in Romans 8:33 says that none of us can do anything to give ourselves a secure standing in the presence of the Supreme Evaluator?

4. Describe an event that greatly encouraged you when you realized that someone was for you, desiring your success.

5. A lot of people are only consumers. They spend their lives in feverish grasping, scrambling to "get it all" here and now. But we do not need to live such desperate and futile lives. Why? (See Romans 8:32.)

6. Baptized into the name of the Father, Son, and Holy Spirit, we are now united with Christ. This brings us not only a challenge but also a source of confidence. What are these? (See Mark 1:15; Romans 8:39.)

Vision

During This Week

1. Analyze a TV commercial or soap opera. List three false views of life you see presented that you recognize as contrary to God's will for human life.
2. Reflect on these words of the 19th-century theologian C. F. W. Walther: "The Law must first crush the sinner's heart before the sweet comfort of the Gospel is applied to him. But from this fact the inference must not be drawn that the sinner *may* not believe. It is forever true that any person may believe at any time. Even when he has fallen into the most grievous sin and, realizing suddenly that he has forsaken God, rises with a crushed heart, he may believe [forgiveness is still there for him to receive]." (*The Proper Distinction Between Law and Gospel* [Dau translation, CPH, 1929], p. 373.)
3. Choose a verse from Luther's "A Mighty Fortress Is Our God" to sing or meditate upon at the beginning of each day.

Closing Worship

Pray together:

Dear Heavenly Father, temptations sometimes appear incredibly difficult to us, for we are not great people of faith. Remind us that the temptations and hardships we find most heart wrenching become the opportunities for blessings unforeseen to come into our lives. Hold before us Your Scripture promises that You always provide us with victory.

Teach us anew that we are so precious in Your sight that You were willing to sacrifice Your Son for us. We return this day to Jesus, our Victor, the Provider for our greatest need. We praise You that in Him we are "more than conquerors." Amen.

Scripture Lessons for Next Sunday

Read Genesis 28:10–22; Romans 5:1–11; and Mark 8:31–38 in preparation for the next session.

Session 2

The Second Sunday in Lent

(Genesis 28:10–22; Romans 5:1–11; Mark 8:31–38)

Focus

Theme: *Losing Life to Find It*

Law/Gospel Focus

We sometimes suffer as a result of our sin. Yet Jesus Christ, our Intercessor, experienced a depth of suffering we need never endure. He has brought God's redeeming love to us and reconciled us with the holy God. Through His Word and Sacrament, Christ invites us to follow Him and strengthens us for a life of self-giving. So to follow Christ is to discover everlasting glory.

Objectives

That by the enabling power of the Holy Spirit working through God's Word, we will
1. daily acknowledge with joy and praise that God has given us Jesus Christ as the sure way to everlasting glory;
2. appreciate His church as the place where God still reveals to us continued grace and blessing in Word and Sacrament; and
3. desire to follow Christ in a self-giving life.

Opening Worship

Sing or pray together "How Blessed Is This Place, O Lord."

> How blessed is this place, O Lord,
> Where You are worshiped and adored!
> In faith we here an altar raise
> To Your great glory, God of praise.

Here let Your sacred fire of old
Descend to kindle spirits cold;
And may our prayers, when here we bend,
Like incense sweet to You ascend.

Here let the weary one find rest,
The troubled heart, Your comfort blest,
The guilty one, a sure retreat,
The sinner, pardon at Your feet.

Here Your angelic spirits send
Their solemn praise with ours to blend,
And grant the vision inly giv'n
Of this Your house, the gate of heav'n.

Introduction

A gardener does not keep seeds in a paper bag under the sink. Rather, by scattering the seeds at the proper time of year, the gardener is rewarded with a beautiful garden. This is true with life in general. Life, like love, survives and thrives only as it is scattered in self-giving.

The Son of God lost His life upon a cross. But in losing it He entered life eternal. Similarly, Christ's followers are called upon in faith to lose their lives for His and His Gospel's sake. In so doing we find life's true purpose—life itself.

In 2 Timothy 1:14 St. Paul urges Timothy, "Guard the good deposit that was entrusted to you—guard it with the help of the Holy Spirit who lives in us."

1. Often when called upon to guard something valuable we may be inclined to hide it. How might you guard a large sum of money or a precious jewel?

2. The deposit that St. Paul calls upon Timothy to guard is the Gospel—the Good News of Jesus Christ crucified for our sins. How do we guard this most precious and valuable gift so it is not lost?

3. How is the "good deposit" entrusted to Timothy and to us greater than a precious jewel or a large sum of money?

Inform

The Old Testament lesson, Genesis 28:10–22, records a turning point in Jacob's life. Fleeing from his brother Esau whom he had tricked out of his birthright, the fearful and tired Jacob camped for the night. God came to comfort him in a dream, speaking in words much the same as those of the promise He had given Abraham. Jacob saw a ladder that God Himself set up from earth to heaven. He called that place the "House of God." In gratitude Jacob promised solemnly that he would worship and serve this God faithfully all his days.

The Epistle lesson, Romans 5:1–11, describes blessings that result when God the Judge declares us not guilty on account of Jesus Christ who died for us. Although we are sinners, we stand in a relationship of peace with God. We need not fear His wrath on Judgment Day. We can rejoice despite present suffering, secure in the promise that Jesus won our salvation.

In the Gospel lesson, Mark 8:31–38, Jesus asks His disciples to summarize their impressions of Him. Peter, speaking for them, confesses that Jesus is the promised Messiah. But they do not yet understand that as the Messiah, Jesus must, as the Son of Man, endure suffering and death prior to His victorious resurrection. When Jesus sets them straight, they are thrown into confusion. Moments after his confession, Peter refuses to accept Jesus' suffering as His path to glory. Then Jesus tells them all that they must walk the way of suffering and rejection. For those who follow Christ, the cross comes before the crown.

1. What do you consider the most amazing part of Jacob's dream?

2. What did Jacob do when he awoke from his sleep? Why? (See Genesis 28:17.)

3. The people for whom Jesus died are described in two shocking ways. What are they? (See Romans 5:6.)

4. Jesus' death has given us access to all the treasures of heaven. List some of these. (See Romans 5:1, 3–5, 9–11.)

5. The Gospel is not merely a message preached by Jesus, but in Mark 8:31–38 it is identified with Jesus Himself. What words express this identification?

6. Where in Mark 8:31–38 does Jesus drive home His point by using business language?

7. Who, finally, loses His life? (See Mark 8:35.)

Connect

1. People "join" churches for various reasons. List some. Based on the Old Testament lesson, explain why we are "members" of the church.

2. One minute Peter had been led by God to confess the true nature of Jesus (compare to Matthew 16:17), then the next minute he was thinking like an unbelieving man and expressing the thoughts of Satan! This serves as a warning to us also. What can we learn?

3. "To deny" is a courtroom term in which a witness disavows any association with another. "To deny oneself" (Mark 8:34) means that one has broken with all self-interest. Can you think of a situation in which you may have to do this?

4. As you have visited cemeteries or funeral chapels, what have you observed of the ways in which people try to ease their fear of death? Are the images in the hymn stanza comforting or disturbing to you? Why?

> I fall asleep in Jesus' wounds,
> There pardon for my sins abounds;
> Yea, Jesus' blood and righteousness
> My jewels are, my glorious dress,
> Wherein before my God I'll stand
> When I shall reach the heavenly land.

Vision

During This Week

1. Make cards for people who are terminally ill or in a nursing home. Use ideas from our lessons to illustrate the foundation of Christian hope.
2. Interview an older member of your congregation. Ask why he or she considers the church a "bethel," a house of God.
3. Browse through your hymnal for hymns about justification or hope. Write down one or more insights these hymns give you about the Christian's confidence.

Closing Worship

Pray together:

Dear Heavenly Father, we thank You that in Your great mercy You have set up a ladder from heaven to earth in the person of Your Son, Jesus Christ. By Your Word and Spirit, continue to give us confidence that through Him we enter into Your kingdom now and forever. Help us all, we pray, to build our lives and our hope of eternal salvation on Him. Keep us from trusting in any ladder of self-chosen works and righteousness, for they would crumble under the weight of our sins and the scrutiny of Your holiness. Guard and preserve us on the way to life eternal, and at length send Your holy angels to take us home. Amen.

Scripture Lessons for Next Sunday

Read in preparation for the Third Sunday in Lent the following: Exodus 20:1–17; 1 Corinthians 1:22–25; John 2:13–22.

Session 3

The Third Sunday in Lent

(Exodus 20:1–17; 1 Corinthians 1:22–25; John 2:13–22)

Focus

Theme: *Wise in Christ*

Law/Gospel Focus

God has given us His demands for a holy life consistent with His will. But we reject His authority. Foolishly, we think we possess sufficient power to be captains of our own ships and have enough wisdom to master our own destiny. God in Christ has entered into our lives to lead us out of our slavery to sin. Trusting the message of the crucified Christ, we partake in God's wisdom that brings us safely to our eternal home.

Objectives

That by the enabling power of the Holy Spirit working through God's Word, we will
1. forsake all dependence upon our own ability to seek God's will for our lives based on human wisdom and accomplishments;
2. thank God the Father for revealing to us the divine power and wisdom found in Jesus Christ; and
3. aim to be living proof of the power of God's wisdom by confessing confidently Jesus Christ crucified.

Opening Worship

Sing or pray together the following stanzas of "Jesus, Lover of My Soul."

Jesus, lover of my soul,
Let me to Thy mercy fly
While the nearer waters roll,
While the tempest still is high.
Hide me, O my Savior, hide
Till the storm of life is past;
Safe into the haven guide.
Oh, receive my soul at last!

Plenteous grace with Thee is found,
Grace to cover all my sin.
Let the healing streams abound;
Make and keep me pure within.
Thou of life the fountain art,
Freely let me take of Thee;
Spring Thou up within my heart,
Rise to all eternity.

Introduction

Sometimes we foolishly think we know a great deal when we really don't. On April 15, 1912, the presence of icebergs in the North Atlantic was reported to the captain of the Titanic, the fabled ocean liner on its maiden voyage. He was not very concerned. He had been told that this great ship was "unsinkable." Ultimately, 1512 of the 2224 persons on board perished.

Anyone is a fool who considers himself too wise or too strong to need the message of repentance and faith in Jesus Christ. On Judgment Day, people who lived lives unconnected to Christ will face a resurrection to eternal damnation.

God in His wisdom keeps pointing us and everyone else to Jesus Christ the Law-fulfiller, the one crucified in the place of all lawbreakers. Resting in Him, sinners are placed into the lifeboat that brings them to the shore of resurrection glory.

1. How does God provide you a lifeboat in Christ Jesus?

2. How is the wisdom of the lifeboat provided by God in Christ Jesus often considered foolishness to the world?

Inform

In Exodus 20:1–17 God addresses the children of Israel after the exodus from Egypt. He gives them the Ten Commandments in which He has summarized His will for humankind, starting with and flowing from the fact that He alone is God.

1 Corinthians 1:22–25 reminds us that the heart of Christian preaching—salvation through Christ's cross—scandalizes those who seek God in visible power and sounds foolish to those who depend on human reason to provide humanity with all it needs.

In John 2:13–22 Jesus is presented as the faithful, law-abiding Son of Abraham. He attends the Jewish Passover at Jerusalem's temple. He strongly opposes corruption brought about by those who hoard money and power. Moreover, He Himself would be the new sacrifice (John 1:29) and the new center of worship (John 4:19–24). In Jesus, sinners meet a gracious God.

1. What is surprising about that which precedes God's commandments?

2. How did Paul play on the word "wisdom" in the Epistle lesson? (See Psalm 111:10; Proverbs 3:5–6; and James 1:5.)

3. Paul presents a strange paradox in 1 Corinthians 1:25. What is it? What do you think it means?

4. It was logical for the Jewish religious leaders, as guardians of the Jewish faith, to test anyone who came along claiming to be a prophet. "Jews demand miraculous signs," Paul said (1 Corinthians 1:22). What was the "sign" that Jesus said He would ultimately give them? It turned out to be a "stumbling block" (1 Corinthians 1:23) to them, but it still decisively points to Him as truly being God's Messiah. (Compare Matthew 12:39–40 with John 2:19–22.)

5. Compare the Gospel lesson, especially verse 21, with Malachi 3:1 in the Old Testament and 1 Corinthians 3:16–17 and 12:27 in the New Testament. What is the "foolishness" (by the world's standards) described? What does it mean for you?

Connect

1. Make two lists of admonitions based on the Ten Commandments, one headed *Don't Do* and the other *Do*. What do you think lies behind each of them? Does our world look upon people who try to keep such commands as wise or foolish? Why?

2. What is the connection between the list you made and the reason Jesus came to earth to suffer and die on the cross?

3. The Epistle lesson speaks of wisdom and foolishness. Is Christianity anti-intellectual? Why or why not?

4. What are some of the ways in which we can show that we want to seek God's wisdom and power in Christ?

5. Many people have no difficulty with Jesus as the "babe of Bethlehem" or the great moral teacher of the Sermon on the Mount. But they grow uncomfortable with the Christ of the cross. Why?

Vision

During This Week

1. Many hymns point us to a great deal more than the here and now. Look for such hymns in the hymnal. Take note of the constructive aspects of looking beyond the familiar to some "hidden" wisdom that God teaches us.
2. Examine your checkbook or credit card bill. Circle expenditures you now recognize as unnecessary, although you may have considered them needs at the time. Ask God in prayer to enable you to keep in proper perspective the true needs in your life.
3. Scan the newspaper for some headline that chronicles human foolishness caused by pride. Be warned all over again that pride often comes before a fall.
4. If you watch a TV "soap," take one episode and list which of the Ten Commandments the characters break. Does the soap actually encourage the viewer to break the commandments by not showing the consequences of such disobedience?

Closing Worship

Sing or speak the following stanzas of "One Thing's Needful; Lord, This Treasure."

> Wisdom's highest, noblest treasure,
> Jesus, lies concealed in Thee;
> Grant that this may still the measure
> Of my will and actions be,
> Humility there and simplicity reigning,
> In paths of true wisdom my steps ever training.
> Oh, if I of Christ have this knowledge divine,
> The fulness of heavenly wisdom is mine.
>
> Naught have I, O Christ, to offer
> Naught but Thee, my highest Good.
> Naught have I, O Lord, to proffer
> But Thy crimson-colored blood.
> Thy death on the cross hath death wholly defeated
> And thereby my righteousness fully completed;
> Salvation's white raiments I there did obtain,
> And in them in glory with Thee I shall reign.

Scripture Lessons for Next Sunday

Read in preparation for the Fourth Sunday in Lent the following: Numbers 21:4–9; Ephesians 2:4–10; and John 3:14–21.

Session 4

The Fourth Sunday in Lent

(Numbers 21:4–9; Ephesians 2:4–10; John 3:14–21)

Focus

Theme: *The Focus That Inspires Hope*

Law/Gospel Focus

Our hope is our conviction that, although our willful sins often cast us down, Christ in His own time will raise us up. Whether in conversion or in the repentance that marks our ongoing walk in His Word, we look in hope to no one and nothing but Jesus our Savior. He is divine Grace and Mercy in human flesh. He is both the content and the author of our saving faith.

Objectives

By the enabling power of the Holy Spirit working through God's Word, we will

1. desire to be rid of all that distracts us from focusing on God's grace and the riches obtained for us by Jesus' work;
2. take time daily to focus upon God's grace in Christ found in Scripture so our faith may have the upward, forward look called hope; and
3. express our joy in Christ's gift of forgiveness by speaking of Him to those still engulfed in spiritual darkness.

Opening Worship

Sing or speak together the following stanzas of "Lift High the Cross":

Refrain:
Lift high the cross, the love of Christ proclaim
Till all the world adore His sacred name.

O Lord, once lifted on the glorious tree,
Raise us, and let Your cross the magnet be. *Refrain*

So shall our song of triumph ever be:
Praise to the Crucified for victory! *Refrain*

Introduction

Human beings have been able to accomplish a lot through persistence and hard work. None of us would necessarily want a life without modern means of travel and the medicines that help to alleviate physical pain. However, human striving cannot produce answers to questions regarding the ultimate meaning and purpose of human existence.

Only a fool would drive an expensive car without first consulting the owner's manual or travel to a faraway destination without consulting a map. On our journey through life, God provides us with a manual and a map that unleash His power for salvation in our lives. The great mansion that is our ultimate home has doors that He alone opens from the inside.

Despite our struggles—from lonely battles with depression to unemployment to marital or parental problems—we Christians walk with confidence. Looking to Scripture, which focuses upon Jesus Christ, we see the riches He has in store for us. This creates the hope that enables us to walk confidently through life, accomplishing marvelous deeds by His grace.

1. What have you been able to accomplish through persistence and hard work?

2. Give evidence from your life or the lives of others of the futility of seeking answers to spiritual matters through persistence and hard work.

3. God has provided the answers to all spiritual matters in Scripture. What comfort does this fact give you as you face daily life?

Inform

Read the following summaries of the Scripture lessons for the Fourth Sunday in Lent.

Numbers 21:4–9—This is a story of sin, for a nation rebelled against God and had to be punished. God sent poisonous snakes that bit the people so that many died. But the story is also one of divine rescue, for Moses interceded for the people and God provided a remedy. He told Moses to make a brass serpent and lift it up on a pole for all to see. Any stricken person who looked at the uplifted serpent would immediately be healed. Thus, we have a story of faith: when the people looked in faith, they were saved.

Ephesians 2:4–10—God's inspired spokesman, the apostle Paul, comforts the church. Through faith in the once-crucified Jesus, who is now lifted to His eternal glory, all who are united with Him share in His riches. Christians are gifted with God's grace, given new spiritual life by Him, exalted, kept safely in His hands, and energized by Him that He may work through them. Thus, as God's masterpieces, they can even now exhibit the nature of their heavenly life.

John 3:14–21—The evangelist relates a night conversation of Jesus with one of Judaism's top theologians, Nicodemus. Jesus uses the episode recorded in Numbers 21:4–9 as an earthly illustration of the need of sinners, who without Him are all subject to spiritual death. All who look to Jesus in faith receive healing that brings eternal life.

1. What did the Israelites do that indicated their repentance of their sins?

2. Which of the following was God's solution to the "snake" problem?
   - Pass antiserpent laws
   - Climb a pole
   - Kill the serpents
   - Pretend they were not there
   - Form a committee to do research
   - Do what Isaiah 45:22 says

3. Describe a parallel between the brass serpent lifted up on a pole and the Son of God lifted up on a cross.

4. The brass serpent was raised high above the camp, drawing the attention of people everywhere so that they might receive health and salvation. Which word of Jesus in John 3:15 parallels this?

5. All that the Son of God accomplished upon this earth was done in our place and for our benefit. Therefore, the victorious life of Christ previews our life as well. What words in Ephesians 2:4–5 affirm this marvelous truth?

6. What four-letter word in John 3:14 stresses that if anyone is to receive eternal life, it can come about only through a great sacrifice and that the Son of God is the only one who made that sacrifice?

7. What verse in John 3:14–21 stresses that no one can be neutral toward Jesus as their Savior?

8. God's condemnation falls upon the world not because of its political, social, and moral evils, but because of what? (See John 3:19.)

Connect

1. Which bad characteristics of the wandering Israelites do we sometimes exhibit, even though God has blessed us with great gifts?

2. Where are crosses used in today's culture to make a mockery of what Christ's cross means to Christians?

3. Although we are by nature "sinful and unclean," that is not the only description that applies to us. At the same time, through Christ, how are we also described? (See Ephesians 2:10.)

4. Instead of our "grave" clothes, Christ supplies us with new "grace" clothes. How can and do we show others our new clothes?

Vision

During This Week

1. Make a list of anxieties. Present them to God through prayer.
2. Search your hymnal for hymns that exalt God's grace. Take one of those hymns and open and close your day by meditating upon its stanzas.
3. Meditate upon the following Bible passages that assure you of God's aid:

   "Surely I am with you always, to the very end of the age" (Matthew 28:20).

   "Greater love has no one than this, that he lay down his life for his friends" (John 15:13).

Closing Worship

Sing together the following stanza from "My Faith Looks Trustingly."

> My faith looks trustingly
> To Christ of Calvary,
> My Savior true!
> Lord, hear me while I pray,
> Take all my guilt away,
> Strengthen in every way
> My love for You.

Pray together:

Dear Heavenly Father, we thank You for Your grace in Your gift to us of Your Son Jesus Christ. He finished the work You gave Him to do. Now You have placed before us His cross that answers any charges against us. Let the reception of His cross continue to enrich our churches, homes, and hearts. May the vision of Christ before us keep us from excess sorrow, doubts, and fears. And may His sacrifice and Your love move us to offer to You our hearts, minds, and hands. Amen.

Scripture Lessons for Next Sunday

Read Jeremiah 31:31–34; Hebrews 5:7–9; and John 12:20–33 in preparation for the Fifth Sunday in Lent.

Session 5

The Fifth Sunday in Lent

(Jeremiah 31:31–34; Hebrews 5:7–9; John 12:20–33)

Focus

Theme: *In Giving Is Glory*

Law/Gospel Focus

The human heart is powerless to change its selfishness. But God comes to sinners through the Good News about Jesus to establish a blissful relationship with Him and grant a new spirit within. Through daily reliance upon God's grace, expressed in obedience to His Word, God's people live out His forgiveness. They see themselves as a network of the redeemed, privileged to widen their fellowship by sharing Christ with all those about them.

Objectives

By the enabling power of the Holy Spirit working through God's Word, we will
  1. recognize the sin centered in our rebellious hearts that refuses to obey God's will and to give Him glory;
  2. thank God for the gift of Christ who died for us and for His transforming power in our hearts that we receive through the Gospel; and
  3. use every opportunity to glorify God by pointing to Jesus as the world's only Savior.

Opening Worship

Sing or speak together "Come to Calvary's Holy Mountain."
> Come to Calv'ry's holy mountain,
> Sinners, ruined by the fall;
> Here a pure and healing fountain

> Flows for you, for me, for all,
> In a full perpetual tide,
> Opened when our Savior died.
>
> Take the life that lasts forever;
> Trust this soul-renewing flood.
> God is faithful; God will never
> Break His covenant of blood,
> Signed when our Redeemer died,
> Sealed when He was glorified.

Introduction

In many churches a small plaque inside the pulpit, visible only to the preacher, says, "We would see Jesus." What matters is not the preacher's skill but the content of the message he brings—the Gospel that exalts the self-giving Christ.

A tourist was visiting churches while traveling. He told an usher one week, "What a wonderful preacher you have here!" The next Sunday he went to another church. This time as he left he said, "My, what a wonderful Savior you have here." That is quite a difference!

It can be a far-reaching difference. Any preacher's sermon is not really over until it is lived out in the lives of those who hear it. Wherever we Christians are, it is always music to our ears to hear, "What a wonderful Savior you have!"

1. How are the tourist's statements different?

2. Why is it important for people to echo the words, "My, what a wonderful Savior you have here," as they leave worship or Bible study?

Inform

Read the following summaries of the Scripture lessons for the Fifth Sunday in Lent.

Jeremiah 31:31–34—Jeremiah had pronounced the Lord's judgment on faithless and rebellious Judah. But here he added that God, the ever-faithful Rescuer of His people, also speaks a word of forgiveness in the new covenant that He Himself would establish through the Messiah.

Hebrews 5:7–9—Addressing Jewish Christians who were thinking to escape Roman persecution by returning to the "legal" religion of Judaism, the writer points out the superiority of Christ. Jesus is the superior High Priest both in His teaching and in the sacrifice He offered. But His attitude is as important as His actions. As shown by His agonizing prayer in Gethsemane, Jesus, our High Priest, understands suffering and is not indifferent toward those who ask for help.

John 12:20–33—As Jesus the Messiah closes His three-year ministry He knows what awaits Him on Golgotha—the cross. When some non-Jews want to see Him, He speaks about the worldwide benefits of His sacrifice. His total self-giving stands in contrast with the self-willing and self-serving goals of Satan and sinners. Jesus disciples did not yet appreciate the cross. Yet from Jesus' giving up His own life, new and eternal life would spring up for all the world. In this, God is glorified.

1. What kind of "knowledge" does God intend all people to have of Him (Jeremiah 31:34)?

2. Even in Old Testament times, the only way of salvation was through the forgiveness of sins. God was treating people in a "New Testament" way (see Jeremiah 31:34), as repeatedly He promised and gave salvation to helpless sinners through the years. When and how did the New Testament come to its fullness? Skim Hebrews 8:8–9:17; also consult Matthew 26:26–28 and Luke 22:19–20.

3. Which words in Jeremiah 31:34 affirm that God's new covenant is available to everyone?

4. Hebrews 5:8 speaks of the Son learning obedience. This is a difficult concept for Christians to understand. What does it mean?

5. "Once made perfect" (Hebrews 5:9) means made "mature" or "complete." Certainly the Son of God Christ was perfect; at no time was He rebellious or disobedient. But as the Son of Man, our great High Priest, suffering and obedience matured Him for a special purpose. What purpose? (Compare John 12:24 with Hebrews 5:9.)

6. Since the Bible stresses that nothing we do can save us, what does Hebrews 5:9 mean in saying that Jesus is the Savior of "all who obey Him"?

7. Jesus as the Lamb of God who takes away not just some sins but the "sin of the world" is a major theme of John the Gospel writer (1:29). (Compare John 3:16; 6:33, and 8:12.) How is this shown in the Gospel lesson for today?

8. According to John 12:28, something of God was revealed when the Father sent Jesus into the world and raised Him from the dead. What? (See John 11:4, 40.)

Connect

1. How do you picture Jesus of Nazareth? Has your picture of Him changed as a result of Hebrews 5:7–9? Explain.

2. Our culture of theme parks, recreational vehicles, and camcorders pursues fun and pleasure with great intensity. Despite that, our world is full of misery and the lack of self-esteem. What paradox lies at the heart of this problem?

3. Describe some concrete examples of losing one's life for Christ's sake.

Vision

During This Week

1. Create a picture of Jesus. Then ask one or two children to create a picture of Jesus and describe it. Then share your picture.
2. "Hate" your life in this world (John 12:25) by choosing to do some activity with a husband or child that they like but you don't (e.g., wife going to an athletic game with her husband; husband going to the mall with his wife).
3. Write your own prayer based on insights from the three Scripture passages. Pray it on behalf of an individual who you know needs encouragement.

Closing Worship

Pray together:

O heavenly Father, we thank You for Jesus Christ our compassionate High Priest and His perfect obedience on our behalf and in our place. Through Him, You declare Your almighty power to forgive our wickedness and remember our sins no more. When we are suffering, help us to remember His suffering and the certainty of His gift of eternal life to us. Empower us today to glorify You by a life of compassion that draws others to Jesus.

Savior, teach me day by day
Love's sweet lesson to obey.
Sweeter lesson cannot be,
Loving You who first loved me.
Amen.

Scripture Lessons for Next Sunday

Read for the Sixth Sunday in Lent the following: Zechariah 9:9–10; Philippians 2:5–11; and Mark 14:1–15:47.

Session 6

The Sixth Sunday in Lent

(Zechariah 9:9–10; Philippians 2:5–11; Mark 14:1–15:47)

Focus

Theme: *The Master's Mind*

Law/Gospel Focus

In our self-absorbed, approval-seeking lives, we want to surround ourselves with those who satisfy our need for compliments. The Son of God left heaven not to be served, but to serve the needs of others. While fully divine, in deep humility He set aside His divine power as He endured the vilest of treatment, which culminated on the cross where He was forsaken by God in our place. As a result, God exalted Him as the bringer of salvation and Lord of all.

Objectives

That by the enabling power of the Holy Spirit working through God's Word, we will
1. daily repent of the sin of selfishness;
2. rejoice that Jesus is Lord over all creation and of our salvation, despite our hesitancy to acknowledge Him; and
3. be alert to spot the unspoken needs of people we meet, that we may tell them of the peace bestowed by the living Lord for troubled hearts.

Opening Worship

Sing or pray together the following stanzas of "How Sweet the Name of Jesus Sounds."

How sweet the name of Jesus sounds
In a believer's ear!
It soothes our sorrows, heals our wounds,
And drives away all fear.

I praise in weakness from afar—
How cold my warmest thought!
But when I see You as You are,
I'll praise You as I ought.

Till then I would Your love proclaim
With ev'ry fleeting breath;
And may the music of Your name
Refresh my soul in death!

Introduction

In times of both war and peace, the idea of one world government has been debated during the last hundred years. As the 21st century begins, our planet is increasingly recognized as a global village linked through sophisticated communications and tied together by world-famous products.

But despite technological advancements, the earth still does not have true peace, either for individuals or for entire nations. The question arises again and again: From where and when can lasting peace come? This goal eludes even the sharpest of intellects.

Today's Scripture readings reveal the one whose surprising actions established a kingdom that now provides an inner peace. One day He will reveal to us and in us a visible glory without limits, but not as we can imagine. Today's lessons give us an insight into the Master's Mind.

1. Describe a mastermind.

2. How might a mastermind differ from the Master's Mind?

Inform

Read the following summaries of the Scripture lessons for the Sixth Sunday in Lent.

Zechariah 9:9–10 prophetically describes Judah's future king. He surprises the world as He comes in humility, riding upon a donkey's colt. As Servant-King, He looks to no human power to build His kingdom, but relies on God alone. Through Him, God would conquer the world in a way that establishes peace based on righteousness and salvation for sinners.

Philippians 2:5–11 describes the two states of Jesus the God-Man after the incarnation, humiliation, and exaltation. Though still remaining God and having all divine power even according to His human nature, He humbly refrained from using His divine prerogatives. Unlike Satan (who glories in himself—see Genesis 3:5; Matthew 4:9), Christ Jesus the Servant-Savior sought not to enhance His own glory but to serve the needs of corrupted humanity. He supplies His followers not only with a pattern for living which they can contemplate, but also the power to put it into practice. Paul invites Christians to adopt the mind of Christ as they serve others in His name.

Mark 14:1–15:47 describes the shameful events connected to Jesus' crucifixion. Betrayal, cowardice, misunderstanding, insult, and unbelief accompany Christ to the cross. Despite it all, though, Jesus remains the solitary suffering Savior. Totally in control although abandoned by many, He drinks the cup of God's judgment upon humanity's sin (15:33–39). He completed salvation for sinners.

1. God's ways often are not our ways. What is so shocking about the way Jesus displays His kingship? (See Zechariah 9:9; Mark 14:48, 60–61; 15:31–32.)

2. On the basis of the Old Testament and Epistle lessons, list three titles or names that apply to the Savior.

3. Jesus' work of salvation is even much grander than saving us—as marvelous as that is. What is His ultimate purpose? (See Ephesians 1:6, 12, 14.)

4. What was the last surprising thing that Jesus and His disciples did in the upper room before starting out for the Mount of Olives?

5. Jesus is Lord over all situations, including the events connected to His cross. How does this truth come through in the long lesson from Mark? (See especially Mark 14:17–21, 22–25, 27–31, 48–49; 14:61; 15:4–5; 15:37.)

6. Upon the cross Jesus experienced the very suffering of hell. He took God's infinite wrath against sin into Himself so His followers would not have to. What words of Jesus express this mysterious but marvelous event?

Connect

1. Charles Lamb, one of England's greatest essayists, wrote: "If Shakespeare would come into this room, we would all arise. If Christ came in, we would all fall down at His feet." The church believes that Jesus is Lord of the whole world. Name specific occasions or events that appear to conflict with this claim.

2. Sometimes we today judge Peter harshly for the way he acted on the night before Jesus' crucifixion. Yet we too must confess that we are guilty of the same sorts of things. How?

3. God's ways are indeed not our ways. Discuss: Sinners want to take the place of God, but Christ saved us by taking our place. Whereas we want to be exalted, He was humbled—and so He became our Lord.

4. To call Jesus "Lord" is to say something about ourselves. These words form a pledge of personal commitment. Suggest what it means today for you to confess Jesus as Lord. What concrete action does it imply for your daily work or for family life?

5. Mentoring is recognized as a powerful tool in education. Paul invited the Philippians to adopt the mind of Christ. What attitudes, therefore, need to be renounced? What mind-set or outlook replaces them?

Vision

During This Week

1. Write a paragraph about someone you consider a model of humility. Then send that person a thank-you note.
2. Make cards with Scripture quotations to give to people who are ill or in a nursing home.
3. Visit a lonely person. After the visit, write down what you learned about the person. Pray for your friend during the week.

Closing Worship

Pray together:
Jesus! Oh, how could it be true,
A mortal man ashamed of You?
Ashamed of You, whom angels praise,
Whose glories shine through endless days?
(From the hymn "Jesus! Oh, How Could It Be True.")

Lord Jesus Christ, our glorious King, we are not ashamed of You—even when You appear among us wearing but a crown of thorns. We praise You as our King of kings and Lord of lords. How could we disown You and claim another as our Savior, Redeemer, Ruler, and Head of the church? We pray, remain with us always as "Jesus," as our only Rescuer and Savior. Amen.